Havana & Varadero Travel Guide

Attractions, Eating, Drinking, Shopping & Places To Stay

Olivia Phillips

Table of Contents

Havana

Havana is the capital of Cuba and is one of the Caribbean's largest and most exciting cities. The city is divided into the districts of Old Havana, Havana Central, Vedado and Miramar. Havana is a Caribbean centre for trade and commerce with Cuban cigars being its most famous export. More than a million tourists come to Havana annually.

Havana was founded by the Spanish in the early 15th century. Fortresses were built along the coast to keep away the French and pirates who were constantly attacking its seaports. The forts were built by the Spanish and trading relations were developing with the West Indies. With trade booming in the 17th century, migrants started to flow to Havana. Today, visitors can visit some of the forts.

Culture

Havana is the cultural capital of Cuba with interesting palaces, museums, churches, public squares, musical and art festivals. The Old Havana region was restored recently and offers a number of new attractions. Various cultural festivals and activities are held annually with most available for free.

Cinema was historically popular in Havana but almost all of the movie theatres in Havana were closed down due to a lack of resources. The locals refer to Havana as a cemetery of theatres. Unfortunately it is has also become a cemetery of markets and shops – but perhaps the more fascinating because of this. However, times are changing for the better.

Major festivals in Havana include the International Jazz festival, International Ballet Festival, International Film Festival, and the Cigar Festival. The Jazz festival features art, music and dance and Cuban Jazz is very popular here. Other important festivals include the International Book Fair, the May Theater and the Havana Carnival.

The Ballet festival is famous not only in Havana but in many other cities in Cuba. It attracts many famous ballet dancers from around the world. The festival started in 1960 and was made official in 1974. Many visitors from home and abroad visit Havana to attend. It is non-competitive in nature and is open to all.

Cuba is famous worldwide for its cigars and they are often regarded as the best cigars in the world. Smaller trade shows, fairs and seminars focusing on the cigar industry, the production of cigars and their distribution are held on a regular basis.

Climate & When to Visit

Havana is a warm country. It enjoys a tropical climate that is wet during the summer but mostly dry during the winter months. Rain falls in abundance and the temperature is constant year round at 24° Celsius from January to December. Rainfall fluctuates with a high amount of rainfall occurring during the months of June, July, September and October. Humidity is high and almost the same all throughout the year.

For more information see:
http://www.wordtravels.com/Cities/Cuba/Havana/Climate

Location & Orientation

Havana is the capital of Cuba and is located on the Caribbean coast. It is divided into a number of main districts including Vedado, Old Havana and Miramar, a newer residential area that was started in the late-1920s. Miramar is home to bureaucrats and has larger homes. Diplomats and foreigners typically live here.

Old Havana city is significantly unchanged from the time before the 1959 Revolution that brought Fidel Castro to power and is divided into various areas including Playa, Centro Habana, Marianao, Plaza de la Revolución, Guanabacoa, Regla, La Habana del Este, San Miguel del Padrón, La Habana Vieja, Guanabacoa, Boyeros, San Miguel del Padrón, La Lisa, Boyeros, Diez de Octubre, Cerro, La Lisa, El Cotorro and Arroyo Naranjo.

Sightseeing Highlights

El Capitolio

Calle Prado (between Dragones and Calles San Jose)
Centro Habana
Havana, Cuba
+ (53) 7 860 3411
http://www.nnc.cubaweb.cu/historia/historia26.htm

The nations Capital building, also popularly known as the El Capitolio and is currently home to the Cuban Academy of Sciences. The building was constructed in 1926 and completed in 1929 and is one of the tallest buildings in Havana.

The building was started before this as a botanical garden and was converted into the Villanueva Station in 1839. Later in the year 1925 a new design for the building was ordered which was completed by 1929. It was named the Palace for Congress or the **El Palacio del Congreso.**

After Castro's communist revolution took place in 1959, the building was used as the headquarters of the Ministry of Science, Technology and Environment. The building is surrounded by gardens that were designed by a French landscaper. The beautiful palm trees in the garden enhance the surroundings of the El Capitolio.

Designated as a site of historical significance by UNESCO, El Capitolio is often compared to the US Capitol building in terms of its architecture. The interior of the building has beautiful marble flooring, stone stairways and a statue representing the Republic of Cuba. The building has three bronze doors with 17 granite iconic columns.

The building is currently under renovation, and is used as a convention center. Various other wings within the building are used for holding art exhibitions, activities and other forms of cultural entertainment. The entrance fee for adults is $3.25 and children under 12 receive free admission. El Capitolio is located in Central Havana and is open from 9am to 6pm, except on Sundays.

Museum of the Revolution & Granma Memorial

Calle Refugio 1
Between Zulueta and Calles Monserrate
Havana, Cuba
+ (7) 862 4092/3/4

Cuba's Museum of the Revolution and the Granma Memorial pays tribute to its current and former leaders who sacrificed their lives in Cuba's freedom and in the 1959 Revolutionary war. It consists of art exhibits, historical photos and propaganda, memorabilia, architectural beauty, airplanes, trucks and spy planes. The motorboat that carried Fidel Castro and his colleagues to the island from Mexico in 1959 is also on display at the Museum.

The museum also shows relics, artifacts, photographs and documents from the Cuban Revolution. Also look for the tank used by Fidel Castro during the Cuban Revolution at the Bay of Pigs battle in 1961 as well as bullet holes in the main interior wall from the storming of the buildings by Castro's troops. The interior of the building is a replica of Versailles's Hall of Mirrors in Paris.

The museum takes about an hour to complete a tour. It is a treasure trove for visitors who are interested in learning about the history of the Cuban Revolution. The museum also offers a unique perspective on the beliefs of Fidel Castro and Che Guevara, two of the most prominent Communist revolutionaries of Cuban history.

Guided tours are often conducted by government officials or payrolled students determined to present you with pro-Cuba / anti-America propaganda. As such they can be quite amusing.

The admission fee for a tourist is $5.40. You can take a guided tour for an additional cost of $2.15. Admission is free for children under the age of 12. The Museo de la Revolución and Memorial Granma is open everyday from 10 am to 5 pm.

Havana Cigar Factories

Fábrica Corona

20 de Mayo #520
e/ Marta Abreu y Línea
Cerro, Havana
+ 07 - 873-0131

Fábrica Partagás

Calle Industria #502
e Dragones y Barcelona
Habana Vieja
+ 07 - 862-0086 or 878-4368

Premium cigars were first made in Havana and several cigar factories can be found here. Only two cigar factories welcome visitors and are well worth visiting. These two are the **Partagas Factory (Fábrica Partagás)** and the **Corona Factory (Fábrica Corona)**.

Visitors here will experience the earthly, intoxicating and pungent aroma of unlit cigar tobacco and see the workers in action. In the tropical heat and while taking in the smell of tobacco one can see the busts of founding father Jose Marti and pictures of Che Guevara and Fidel Castro occupying space on the walls.

In most of the cigar factories in Havana, men are seen doing the task of bunching while women give a hand in rolling. In Cuba the torcedore or the one making the cigar is seen using two binder leaves instead of a single large leaf. But one thing that is special to Havana's cigar factories is the presence of the draw testing machines. These machines have helped in greatly reducing the draw problem that had once plagued the Cuban cigars.

Cigar production has declined in Cuba but you should not miss a trip to a Havana cigar factory. Tour prices are 10 CUC per head (about $11.50). Prices are set by the government, as is common in Cuba. Both the factories are open from Monday to Friday from 9 am to 11 am and then again from 12 noon to 3 pm.

Parque Histórico Morro & Cabaña

Carretera de la Cabaña
Havana
+7/862-0617 for La Cabaña
+7/863-7063 for El Morro

The Parque Histórico Morro y Cabaña is a historical military park which was built in the early 16th century by Spanish invaders. It is a fort which was built to be used to prevent the French and buccaneer pirates from entering the city. This military fort was set at the entrance to Havana Harbor, which was an important trade port.

This historic monument has been serving as a museum of forts and military barracks for many years. It is divided into two major fortresses, namely the **Fortaleza de San Carlos de la Cabaña** and the **Castillo Del Morro**.

Built in the year 1589, the Morro Castle was a major part of Cuban history and was used to defend the city from naval invasions and pirate attacks. The museum holds a military barracks serving as exhibition rooms. The Castillo Del Morro is a place of great interest to visitors. There are also a number of bars and restaurants located nearby where you can spend some time after completing your visit.

Fortaleza de San Carlos de la Cabaña is located nearby and the original purpose of the fortress was to prevent the British from invading Cuba. A museum holds various mementos and warships. The Comandancia de Che Guevara is one of the most notable exhibition halls and was used by Che Guevara to penetrate the fort during the 1959 Revolution. Don't forget to check out the Cuban cigar shops which are located here. The entry fee for adults is $5.40.

The Parque Histórico Militar El Morro-La Cabaña is located in Carretera de La Cabaña, Habana Del Este. La Cabana is open from 10 am to midnight everyday and El Morro is open from 8 am to 8 pm.

Plaza de la Catedral

Calle Empedrado 156
Havana, Cuba
+7-861-7771

The Plaza de la Catedral is one of the best tourist attractions in Havana.

Cut completely from stone, the 18th century San Cristobal de La Habana cathedral is a beautifully constructed building with a variety of wall carvings in its interior walls. The cathedral was recently restored and has much of interest to art lovers. The plaza (square) in front of the cathedral is a great place to people-watch or to relax in the sun.

Another must visit for art lovers is the Centro Wilfredo Lam which houses great art works and is located very close to the cathedral. One of the oldest buildings in Havana, the Museo de Arte Colonial, is also located close to the Centro Wilfredo Lam. The museum contains some of the oldest furniture pieces from the colonial period that were in use in various mansions and palaces. The area is also home to many restaurants, bars, gift shops and shops.

The Palacio Del Conde Lombillo building has a beautiful statue of Antonio Gades, a flamenco dancer. The area was originally a swamp which was renovated to be used as a naval dockyard.

Plaza de la Catedral is located in the Carretera de La Cabaña, Habana Del Este and is open on weekdays. Admission is free. Catholic Mass is held at 9:30 am on Sundays.

Plaza de Armas

Carretera de la Cabaña
Havana, Cuba
+ (7) 863 4950

The Plaza de Armas (Weapons Square) was built during the 17th century and was used as the center of military and religious activity until the middle of the 18th century when it was renovated. It took more than 35 years and millions of dollars to complete the renovation work of Plaza De Armas. After the renovation was completed, the square became a popular meeting spot for the citizens of Havana.

The new name of Cespedes Park was given to the square in memory of the founding father of Cuba. The site is surrounded with churches, official building, cultural palaces and other monuments of architectural brilliance. It is one of the most significant places in Havana. It displays the military past of Cuba including its infamous revolutionary war.

The square was recently added to the UNESCO world heritage list given its historical significance. On the 16th November, many residents of the city walk around the square's ceiba tree (Capok) in the hope that it will bring them luck.

Tourists can also see the City Museum (Museo de la Ciudad). Once a home to some of the highest generals in Cuba, this building has now been converted into the City Museum. The Castillo de le Real Fuerza, the biggest maritime museum of Cuba is also located across the square. The museum is open for long hours on a daily basis and admission fee is $3.

El Malécon

Centro Habana

The El Malecon (seaside promenade) starts from the Castillo de San Salvador de la Punta in Old Havana to the Almendares River, which separates Miramar from Vedado. The total length of the promenade is around 7 kilometers.

Check out some of the old (perhaps crumbling) neo-classical buildings and apartments near to the Malecon. Horse-drawn carriages and 1950's American Cadillac taxis are famous here (and across Havana). This is a great place to people-watch as this is a gathering place for locals and fishermen. This is the best way to feel the "soul" of Havana. The experience of visiting the El Malécon will remain with you for a long time after you return home.

Ernest Hemingway Museum

Finca la Vigía
San Francisco de Paula
(7) 860 9530
http://www.hemingwaycuba.com/finca-la-vigia.html

The Ernest Hemingway Museum which was once the private residence of the renowned American author Ernest Hemingway lies about 15 kilometers from Havana. The Cubans call the museum the Finca Vigia which means the 'lookout house'.

The museum gives visitors an idea of how the author spent his life in Cuba and Hemingway's household furnishings are on display. Visitors will experience the atmosphere of the house that inspired Hemingway to write novels such as The Old Man and the Sea. On display are the 9000 books that comprised the author's personal library. There are also 3000 photographs taken by the author.

The Cubans (and Castro) greatly loved Hemingway and he loved them. Nowadays, the Ernest Hemingway Museum is slipping into a condition of disrepair due to a lack of funds (common to many buildings in Havana). Unfortunately, the high humidity of the region is causing many of Hemingway's papers and books to decay. The Hemingway Foundation (USA) started a restoration project in 2002.

The Ernest Hemingway Museum is located about 9 miles away from Cuba, in the town of San Francisco de Paula. The museum is open six days a week (Monday to Saturday) from 10am to 5pm. It is also open on Sundays from 9am to 1pm. The entrance fee is $3.25 for adults. Children visit free of charge. You can hire a guide for an extra cost.

Recommendations for the Budget Traveler

Places to Stay

People traveling to Havana usually stay in 3 areas - Central Havana, Vedado and Old Havana. Central Havana is a quiet neighborhood and Vedado is filled with nice Casas Particulars (Private home-stays) and large hotels. Check to make sure that your hotel has hot water.

Martha Guests' House

Ave. de los Presidentes No.301
(Between Calle 13 & 15)
Flat 14, 14th floor
El Vedado, Havana
US$ 20 per night

Martha's Guest House is one of the best casa particulars
in a safe area of the city. The rooms are beautifully
decorated and all of them have balconies. The owner of
the guesthouse, Martha, is a very helpful lady who speaks
English. The location is convenient enough for travelers
and is quite peaceful. Breakfast is provided at just 5 CUC
and includes fresh fruit juice, coffee or tea, bread and
scrambled eggs. Other facilities include currency
exchange services, car parking, 24 hour reception, phone
messaging service, towels and linen, lockers, laundry and
mini bar.

Casa Miriam Hostal Colonial

Neptuno #521
e/ Lealtad y Campanario
Habana Centro, Havana
+53 (7) 8784456
$13 per night

Casa Miriam Hostal Colonial offers you a great
opportunity at getting to know Havana better. It was a
recipient of an award by the TripAdvisor website in 2011.

It was also selected as one of the best hostels in Cuba. The building of the hostel was built during 1883 and has been completely restored. The ceilings are as high as 5 meters and the rooms are very sunny and airy. There are spaces for smokers, large balconies and a large common area for guests.

The hostel offers facilities including free local phone calls, free storage of luggage, taxi booking and information about Havana. Laundry services are available at very reasonable rates and a vegetarian dinner and breakfast are offered at nominal prices. All the rooms are equipped with a TV, AC, and comfortable furniture, running hot and cold water, toiletries and a mini fridge. An extra bed comes for 7 CUC.

Hostel Iraida

Calle No. 8 No. 656
Apto 4 Entre Zapata y 27 Vedado,
Havana
$10 / night

Hostel Iraida is located in downtown Havana and is close to many restaurants, hotels, theaters and discos. The Plaza de la Revolucion (where Che Guevara's picture is depicted on the side of a large building) is also located nearby. The facilities offered by the hostel include 24 hour hot water, lockers, fridge, kitchen and DVD players.

Rooms can be shared with 2 or more persons and there are also private rooms available with AC, lockers and fan. Staying in the Hostel Iraida is a great opportunity to meet people from all over the world. It is the ideal place to reduce your transportation costs given its central location and public transportation costs $0.50 to go to many of the main tourist attractions of Havana. Cheap grocery stores are located very near to the hostel.

Casa Zeila

Concordia #255
Apto 301 e/Campanario y Perseverance
Habana Centro, Havana
+53 (7) 8625492
$25 per night

Casa Zeila is a modern, comfortable and clean property with plenty of flowers and plants. Electricity is always available and both hot and cold water are available for 24 hours in a day. It is owned by a very hardworking and friendly lady, Zeila, who speaks English. The property offers laundry and parking services. Rooms are singles or doubles and big and comfortable with TV, AC, ensuite bathrooms, balconies and a fridge. The view offered by the attached balcony will make your stay at Casa Zeila very memorable. The neighborhood is a quiet and calm place and is located just 10 minutes away from the Old Havana area.

Casa Fini

Lugareno 158 apto 1
Entre montor y pozo dulce
Plaza de la Revolucion, Havana
+98 540 03 00
http://www.casafini.net/
$14 per night

Casa Fini is a beautiful hotel located in the city centre. The Capital, one of the biggest tourist attractions of the old city, is located nearby. The hostel is also close to the Central Bus Station and Revolution Square. The neighborhood in which this casa particular is located is one of the oldest districts of Havana and is beautifully paved with cobbled streets. There are many cultural institutions as well as bars located nearby. The facilities offered by the Casa Fini include 24/7 hot and cold water, freezer, breakfast, TV, lunch, kitchen and dinner. A taxi ride from the airport to the Casa Fini costs about 20 CUC.

Places to Eat & Drink

An average meal for one person at government restaurants comes for about $20. It is easy to find a meal at just 10 CUC if you look carefully. Restaurants offering a soup, main course and a dessert between 6 to 10 CUC can be easily found in the El Aljibe suburb in Havana.

Paladar La Tasquita

Calle 27 de Noviembre (Jovellar No.
160) e/ Espada y San Francisco
Havana
873-4916
$15-25

The Paladar La Tasquita is a small restaurant owned by a
family and serves mainly criolla (Spanish) dishes. The
dining space is actually the living room of the family as is
common in Havana. There is nothing glamorous in terms
of the appearance, but the staff is very friendly and the
food is tasty. This is the place to visit to experience typical
Cuban food. Seats are limited so it is important that you
book. The Paladar La Tasquita is open everyday from 12
noon to midnight.

La Casa

30 | Calle 30 #865
e/ 26 y 41 Nuevo
Vedado, Havana 10400
+537 8817000
http://www.restaurantelacasacuba.com/
$10 – 40

The La Casa is located in the Vedado neighborhood and is
stylishly decorated. It is situated in a house which is
designed to look like a building from the pre-
Revolutionary days of the 1950s. The restaurant offers
tasty food and impeccable service.

This is an ideal place to visit for the intimate eating experience it offers to the tourist. La Casa is open everyday from 12 noon to midnight and serves Cuban, Spanish and Italian cuisine. Along with some great food, the restaurant also offers some great views of the sea from the dining room.

El Buganvil

Calle 190, 1501, between Calles 15 & 17,
Playa, Havana
+ (7) 271 4791

El Buganvil is a privately owned restaurant that serves tasty and authentic Cuban food. The most notable dishes are coconut ice cream and the lomo ahumado (smoked pork loin). The lemonade served here is one of the best in the city and the quantity is more then generous. El Buganvil is the place to visit if you want to get a complete Cuban dining experience. The restaurant is open from 12 noon to midnight.

El Bambu

Carretera del Rocio Km 3
Calabazar, Arroyo Naranjo
(at Jardin Botanico Nacional de Cuba)
Havana

The El Bambu is one of the best vegetarian restaurants in Havana. It is located near the Botanical Gardens of Havana and the surroundings are one of the highlights of eating at this place.

The restaurant is mainly located outdoors, so you can check out the beautiful greenery while feasting on some of its tasty vegetarian dishes. The best thing is that a full meal at the El Bambu will cost you 1 CUC. The lunch is styled as a buffet and you can eat as much you like for very little. The highlights of the menu are the salads and the soups.

Din Don

Ave. 11, 7816 entre 78 y 80
Playa, Havana
(7) 203 0445
$3 - $18

Din Don is an Italian and Cuban restaurant that gives great value and is one of the most well known restaurants in the Miramar region. The dining area includes Italian furniture and seats 40 people at one time. The pizzas served here cost just 5 CUC and the pastas cost about 6 CUC. The most famous dishes are the carpaccio at 6 CUC, the Seafood Paella at 8.50 CUC and the Bruschetta at 3 CUC. The excellent choice of desserts include the Torta Din Don which is a cake covered with cream and filled with pear and apple fillings.

Places to Shop

Havana gives you a great opportunity to buy some of the best Cuban rums, cigars and and world-class artwork for good process compared to back home. Almost all of the hotels of the city have a souvenir shop on their premises and prices are charged in CUC. The main shopping hub of the city is Old Havana where you can buy everything from hand-sewn dresses to perfumes and chocolates. Payment is accepted in CUC and credit cards, except for AMEX are accepted at most of the stores.

Shopping Centers

There are a few shopping malls in Havana including Avenida, Tiendas Carlos Tercero and Salvador Allende. All of these malls are filled with cosmetics, shoes and clothes. La Maison located in the Miramar area is the place to buy designer jewelry, cosmetics and clothes.

Markets

The main market of Havana is located close to the Plaza de Catedral and is known as the Artisan Market. This is the place for buying bamboo hats, hand carved sticks and bongo drums (we know you want to). The market is open from 10 am to 8 pm from Wednesdays to Saturdays. There is also a flea market on the El Malecon promenade that is open from 10 am to 8 pm from Sundays to Tuesdays.

Shopping Regions

Cuba is famously known for its cigars. These cigars are expensive outside the country but you can buy them cheaply in Havana. They are locally known as puros or habanos and can be bought from the Calle Oficios, the Casa del Tabaco and the Real Fabrica de Tabacos Partagas cigar factory. Other great buys include Cuban rum and coffee.

Almacenes San Jose Market

Avenida del Puerto corner of Calle Cuba
La Habana Vieja
Cuba
+53 7 864 7793

The Almacenes San Jose Market is located in Old Havana
and is famous for its souvenirs and Cuban artwork. Along
with shopping for attractive cigar boxes and Che Guevara
memorabilia, you can admire the view of the harbor from
the cafes located nearby. The market is open everyday
from 9 am to 5 pm.

Plaza de Armas Book Market

Plaza de Armas
La Habana Vieja, Havana

This is where you need to be if you love reading as well as
bargaining. Several booksellers located near the Plaza de
Armas sell precious and rare books along with Cuban
memorabilia. A day can be enjoyably passed here
browsing at the several bookstalls. The market is open
daily from 10 am to 6 pm.

Varadero

Varadero is a major tourist resort city in Cuba made famous by its beautiful stretch of white sand beach. It is a part of Matanzas province and is located on the northern shores of this Caribbean island. Varadero is a long narrow peninsula stretching into the Gulf of Mexico in the shape of a hockey stick.

The Varadero peninsula was originally inhabited by the indigenous Siboney Indians tribe. Life changed with the arrivals of the Spanish and their African slaves. There are a number of caves which show the area history through their etchings and drawings.

During the mid 16th century the Spanish used the place as a dry dock giving it its present moniker – Varadero – which means dry dock in Spanish. The Spanish Latin American Fleet was also attracted to the peninsula for the salt mines – Las Salinas – which operated till as late as 1961. There is a very strong influence of the Spanish in this area. The language, architecture, and food bear a resemblance to the Spanish. The town of Matanzas was found by the Spanish during the same period. Once called the Athens of Cuba, Matanzas is now known as ciudad de los puentes or the City of Bridges. The rivers Yumuri and San Juan flow though the province. In the late 19th century licenses were given to families to build vacation homes in the area. It was at the same time, in 1887 that Varadero was formally founded.

Varadero was always a favorite destination for swimming for its beautiful blue waters and white sand beaches. It grew in popularity with the coming of tourists in the 1930s. Over time it became a favorite of the elites, attracting rich businessmen, doctors, lawyers, and the cream of the society. In fact, during the 1950s, the working and poorer class Cubans did not get entry to the expensive resorts as guests or patrons. This growing resentment towards the rich and the elite throughout the country triggered the revolution.

After the revolution of 1959 there was a direct impact in the social structure and activity at Varadero. The state started taking control of the assets of the rich and many mansions were made into public institutes and museums. A major park – Parque Central – was built with access to one and all. There were food courts and swimming facilities. The Park became so popular in drawing the public that the place soon started having many social activities like concerts and fairs.

Cuba suffered an economic blow due to a number of embargos and with the disintegration of the USSR in 1990. Tourism once again became one of its major revenue collecting instruments. This prompted lavish expansions in the small town. Large hotel chains started opening their lavish resorts and hotels in the area. The parks, fairs, and festivals that were once the toast of the town slowly fizzled out.

Today, Varadero, with its beach and other natural attractions draws over a million tourists every year. The biggest attraction of Varadero is its beach which is advertised as the 'best beach in the world'. Swanky hotels attract visitors from the US and Canada. Just like in the early 1950s before the revolution, the locals are not allowed as patrons in the resorts, but are only allowed as workers. Natural attractions in the area have also made Varadero a center for cultural activities. The Juan Gualberto Gomez Airport of Varadero has become second only to the airport in Havana in importance and passenger count.

Culture

Varadero has something for all tourists, from snorkeling for the kids to cabarets for the adults. Most of the activities are centered on water and nature.

There are three marinas – the Marlin Marina Darsena, the Marina Gaviota, and the Marina Marlin Darsena de Varadero. These marinas are great for fishing with the Marlin Darsena de Varadero having facilities for larger vessels.

As the names of the marinas suggest, marlins (a type of billfish) are found in the area making it a popular place for fishing. There are a number of operators also organizing snorkeling and scuba diving trips.

The area has a number of natural attractions. The Ambrosio Caves, Bellmar Caves, and the Reserve at Varahicacos provides insight into the early life of the inhabitants in that area. The Parque Central may not have the same glory as in the 1970s but it is still a beautiful place to walk around. Draped with the sea grape trees, the Parque Central houses the biggest Artisan Market in town. The nearby Parque Jososne is also a good place to relax, shop, and have a quick bite.

There a number of monuments and museums which provide a good insight to the history of Varadero. The Museo de Municipal is one such place. The Matanzas port town is also a beautiful place to have a casual stroll. The 400 hundred year old Plaza de la Vigia retains some of the old world charm. Take a ride in a maquina or yank tank, the name given to the big American cars of the 1950s and 1960s that are still plying on the roads of Cuba.

For the sports lovers, Varadero has plenty to offer. The Varadero Golf Club was the first 18-hole golf course in Cuba and is on a beautiful strip of 3.5 km. For the more adventurous, there is biking, horseback riding, and camping.

Varadero has some art galleries and cinemas but the nightlife is dominated by the clubs and the bars. One can experience from the traditional mambo and rumba to the more rebellious disco, cabaret, and hip hop. Popular amongst the clubs – but in no particular order – are Club Mambo, Cabaret Cueva de Pirata, Discoteca La Bamba, and Casa de la Musica.

Location & Orientation

Varadero is located on the north west of the island of Cuba, 140 km east of its capital, Havana. The long peninsula runs for nearly 20 km but is only 1.2 km wide. It is separated from the mainland of Cuba by the Kawama Channel.

Punta Hicacos, which is on the northeastern tip of the peninsula which looks like an inverted hockey stick, is also the northern most point of Cuba. It has an ecological park – Hicacos Park – established in 1974. Varadero is about 150km from Key West, Florida, USA, and about 450 km from the island of Nassau in the Bahamas.

The Juan Gualberto Gomez Airport (IATA: VRA) of Varadero is a single terminal airport but, catering to more than 1.2 million passengers, it handles 25% of Cuba's air passenger traffic. It is about 10 km west of the town and is closer to the town of Matanzas than Varadero. There are a number of airlines operating from the airport with direct connections to quite a few Canadian and European cities including Toronto, Ottawa, London, Lisbon, Zurich, and Amsterdam.

The airport has foreign exchange bureaus but it is better to exchange at other locations as tourists are often short changed. The general practice is to round off to 0.05 CUC, but the airport often rounds off to 10.00 CUC! So it is better to use the service from some outside CADECA – Foreign Exchange Bureau – or banks. Hotels charge an extra 1% to exchange foreign currencies. Taxis and cars are available to travel to and from the airport for about 20 – 30 CUC. One can also negotiate with a tour bus driver or the hotel bus driver for a pick up or drop for about 10 CUC.

By land, Varadero is connected very well with the major Cuban cities like Havana, and Santa Clara. Bus services by Astro - http://www.transtur.cu - and Viazul - http://www.viazul.com/ - connect Varadero with most of the major towns and cities of Cuba. The buses from Havana and Matanzas also stop at the Varadero airport.

For the ones who want to drive, there are a number of rental companies like Havana Autos - http://www.havanautos.com -, Transtur - http://transturhavana.com/ -, and Micar – Tel: 66 85 52. Renting a car is often quite expensive with a standard sedan costing up to $500 for a week. Although Micar has cheaper rentals, the vehicles are mini sized or compact. Some of the major car rentals have their office in the airport. One has to be 21 years of age with a valid driver's license and a year's experience to rent a car.

Within Varadero one can use the Varadero Beach Tour double-decker open-top bus to commute along the peninsula. It runs from 9:30 am to 9:00 pm and a whole day unlimited pass costs 5 CUC. The popular hotel chain Melia Resorts has 3 properties on the peninsula and there is a free shuttle connecting the 3 properties. There are a few public buses that ply on the routes but waiting for one may take a very long time. Many buses do not even have a number and it may be difficult for non Spanish speaker to find where the bus is headed to.

There are a number of companies running Call Cabs or Taxis. The popular ones are run by Transtur (61 34 15), Cuba Taxi (61 05 55), and Transgaviota (61 97 62). Taxis run round the clock and there is no separate night fare. The base rate is 1 CUC and then 1 CUC for every km. The private taxis with yellow license plates are only allowed to carry locals. Coco Taxis – coquitos in Cuban – are shaped liked coconuts, have 2 passenger seats, three wheels, and the motor of a moped. They charge less than a regular taxi with no base rate at the start. Most of the major hotels will have a taxi stand right in front of the hotel.

Caleches – single horse drawn carriage – are also popular in the town. You can rent scooters – 50 cc 2-stroke – from any of the many scooter rentals in town. The longer the rental, the lower the rate. However, it is to be kept in mind that most of these rentals do not allow the scooter to be taken outside town or beyond the tourist areas.

Climate & When to Visit

One does not have to wait for summer in Varadero – it is always summertime! Varadero has a moderate subtropical climate with mainly 2 seasons – dry and wet. Dry season runs from Nov to April and the wet season from May to Oct. As the names suggest, there is a higher precipitation during the wet or rainy season with June and July being the wettest months. Cuba has been hit by a number of hurricanes (tornadoes) although Varadero has mostly escaped the path of calamity. Hurricane season is usually from Jun – Nov, with the highest of chances being around Sep and Oct.

The wet season is hot and very humid with temperatures going up to 30 - 32 degrees Celsius. Precipitation is high but it rarely lasts the whole day. It is suggested to travel with an insect repellent and a good sunscreen lotion during this time of the year.

The dry season has a cooler climate and is the peak time for tourism. Average temperatures hit a high of around 28 – 29 degrees Celsius and a low of around 16 – 17 degrees Celsius. Rains are rare, but since Varadero is on the northern tip of Cuba, there may be chilly winds blowing after sunset.

Sightseeing Highlights

Varadero Beach

The biggest attraction of Varadero is certainly its beach.
With the fall of USSR, Cuba lost its financial support and
tourism, since then, has been a major focus to Cuba.

Varadero, with its milky white beach and clear blue water
has attracted tourists for decades and has become one of
the biggest tourist attractions of Cuba.

The beach runs for about 20 km lined with coco palm
trees and now dotted with swanky and plush resorts.
Varadero has sunny days most of the year thus reducing
the chances that rain will play spoilsport in a vacation.
Most of the resorts are sea facing and provide its guests
with a wide variety of water activities. These include
diving, snorkeling, and sailing. The resorts are equipped
with catamarans, kayaks, and water bicycles aimed at
entertainment for the whole family.

The water at Varadero is not very deep for a long way into the sea making it ideal for snorkeling and water games for families with kids. The water is so clear that one can see the fish through it. The beach also has very good safety features with a flag system that should to be followed at the beach. The flag system works like traffic lights; red flag for no swimming, yellow flag for swimming with caution, and green flag for normal swimming. The flag system is important as the underwater tide can pull a swimmer off route. There are lifeguards who watch the beach closely for the safety of the swimmers, and are available at the lifeguard houses.

Varadero has 3 marinas designed for fishing. Billfish is common in these parts of the world and makes for a great catch. The Marlin Marina Darsena is west of the beach and has deep sea fishing vessels. The famous Gaviota Marina is one of the most important marinas of Cuba and is equipped to handle international vessels and the sailors.

The authorized port for non-Cuban vessels is the Marina Marlin Darsena de Varadero. The Marlin Marina Chapelin is close to Hotel Turquesa, halfway between the Varadero Golf Club and the tip of the peninsula. 5 hours of deep sea fishing costs about CUC 300 for a group of four.

Scuba diving and snorkeling can be done at the Laguna de Maya, which is located halfway between Matanzas and Varadero. One of the premier scuba and snorkeling center is at Barracuda Diving Center. The Cayo Piedro Underwater Park is has cosmetic sunk ships and military equipment. With a lot of sea life around that water body, it also makes for a great dive.

Bottle nosed dolphin shows are popular at the Delfinario (Carretera Las Mortas, Tel: +535 66 80 31) where one can watch dolphin shows and even swim with a dolphin. The tickets are around USD 15 (€ 12) for a 30 min show.

Varadero is also close to a number of other beaches including the Playa Mayor, Playa Larga, Playa Giron, and the Karabelas.

Matanzas Town

Matanzas is a small town to the west of Varadero with a total area of 317 sq km and population of about 150,000. Matanzas, just like Varadero is located on the northern shore of Cuba, in between Varadero and Havana. It is 90 km east of Havana, and about 30 km west from Varadero.

The Juan Gualberto Gomez Airport is 15 km east of Matanzas. The Bay of Matanzas cuts deep into the city and is surrounded by the city on 3 sides. Matanzas has 3 rivers flowing through it, the Rio Yumuri, the Canimar, and the San Juan.

The city of Matanzas, because of its history and geographical features has had a number of names. It is called the City of Bridges as there are 17 bridges that have been built on the 3 rivers flowing through the city. The rivers and the bridges also prompted the nickname of 'Venice of Cuba'. Matanzas has been home to a number of poets and intellectuals earning it the nickname of La Atenas de Cuba or The Athens of Cuba.

Even the very name of the city – Matanzas – comes from a historical incident around the late 15th or early 16th century. Matanzas in Spanish means 'massacre'. It is said that about 30 Spanish soldiers planned to attack the natives in a far off shore. Due to the unavailability of boats, they took the help of the local fishermen who treated them well and agreed to help them. However, in the middle of the river, the fishermen flipped the boats, killing almost all the soldiers except 2, which included the famous Maria Estrada. It is from this massacre that the city got its name.

There were settlements in the city from 1572 but it was officially founded in 1693. It was known as San Carlos y San Severino de Matanzas. In the 16th century Matanzas was popular for the sugar industry – still one of the major industries of Cuba. A large number of African slaves were brought into the country to support the industry.

The population of the slaves grew outnumbering the rest of the population by the 2nd half of the 19th century. Matanzas is also the place of the infamous and rumored Escalera Conspiracy. The city also came in the news when it was bombed by the American navy at the end of the 19th century.

Due to the high population of the African community, who were brought in as slaves, and later, for the immigration of the Portuguese descendants, Matanzas has a strong African and Portuguese influence along with Spanish.

The city has quite a bit of colonial architecture that has been preserved over the years. The Museo Historico Provincial de Matanzas on Milanes Street was completed in 1838. It is a great example of colonial architecture with its ornamental urns and arcades. The Cathedral of San Carlos de Borromeo between Milanes Street and Independent Street was completed in 1735. Other notable structures include the Villa of Bellamur from the 18th century, the Necropolis de San Carlos of the 19th century, and the famous Sauto Theater.

The best way to see all these sites is to cycle around in the streets of Matanzas. For those who would like to take it a little more relaxed, a good option is to rent a coco taxi for a fixed amount and time.

For those who are more into nature, Matanzas has some beautiful natural vegetation. Bird watching is popular in the Yumuri valley. One can also take a boat ride on the Canimar River. One can also go for snorkeling at the Playa Coral, visit the vast vegetation at Cienaga de Zapata, and enjoy the colorful corals at Playa Larga.

Varadero Golf Club

Dupont de Nemours,
Varadero
Tel: 5345 66 84 82
http://www.varaderogolfclub.com

The first 18-hole full-length golf course in Cuba, the
Varadero Golf Club, is a 3.5 km stretch on the peninsula
between the Breezes Bella Costa Hotel and the Melia Las
Americas Hotel. The golf course carries along with it a
piece of history as the club house of the golf club is in the
Xanadu mansion, a colonial structure that is nearly 90
years old. The Varadero Golf Club provides a brilliant
view because of its location and provides a challenging
course with strong ocean winds.

The Xanadu Mansion Golf Club was built in 1927 for the
French American multi millioinaire Irenee Du Pont de
Numours belonging to the famous Du Pont empire. He
built a 4 storey mansion, with 3 terraces and a private
dock and named it Xanadu after the fabled exotic palace
built by Kublas Khan, the legendary Chinese warrior and
conqueror. 5 years later, Du Pont installed the largest
organ in Latin America at a cost of 11000 dollars.
Although the organ was kept at the basement, shafts were
built to carry the music to other parts of the mansion.
Marble and wood came from all corners of the world. The
mansion was completed at a cost of 1.3 million dollars.

The golf course was designed and constructed in 1931, although it had to be completely restored in 1936 after a devastating hurricane had destroyed most of the course within 2 years of its inauguration. On December 12th of 1963, the Las Americas restaurant was opened in the Xanadu Mansion – co-incidentally, in the USA, Mr. Du Pont passed away on the very same day.

Today, the Xanadu Mansion is a 3-storied mansion with a basement that is used as a wine cellar. The ground floor has the lobby and the restaurant; the first floor has luxury hotel rooms for rentals, and the 2nd floor has the Casa Blanca Panoramic Bar.

The beautifully maintained golf club rents out the renowned 'Taylor Made' golf clubs for those who do not bring their own clubs. There are also golf lessons for beginners. A green fee at the club costs about $43.

Day Trip to Havana

The Cuban capital Havana is about 140 km west of Varadero. Many prefer to visit the capital on a day trip from Varadero. There are a number of ways one can get there by road. There is no ferry service available.

The most common public transport service is the Viazul bus service. Viazul runs a shuttle service from most resorts to its bus station at a cost of about 3 CUC. The bus takes about 2.5 – 3 hrs and costs about 10 -12 CUC, one-way.

The bus crosses some beautiful countryside and the tallest bridge in Cuba – the 110 m tall Bacunayagua Bridge. The second option is to use the tour operator of the hotel itself (will cost around $60 - $100 depending on the hotel and its contracted tour operator); they will arrange for the pickup and drop and will, if cost is included, add a guide. The third option is to take a taxi either from the bus station or from the resort itself. Although taking a taxi may be expensive, one has the liberty to choose the time to leave, and get dropped at the preferred location in Havana. A taxi may charge around 80 – 100 CUC one way and will take about 1.5 – 2 hrs. A fourth option is the 'Transfer colectivo' – private shuttle service by travel agencies between Varadero resorts and Havana hotels. They are slightly more expensive than Viazul but much cheaper than taxis.

Once in Havana, one can either rent a coco taxi or simply stroll on foot. For those taking the Viazul bus service, the get off point should be Old Havana just after the bus comes out of the tunnel and enters Havana. The city of Havana, with its crazy traffic and busy roads still retain some old age charm and history through its colonial architecture.

Places to see in Havana include the Plaza de la Revolution / Capitol Building, and Jose Marti Monument. Right behind the Capitolio is the Paratagas Cigar factory which sells authentic Cuban cigars. From the Paratagas, for a stretch of about 6 km one can see the Plazo Park, Museo de la Revolcion (the famous Gramma boat of Fidel Castro is displayed here), Plaza de Armas, Plaza de la cathedral, the Artisans Palace and Artisans Market. The Castillo de Real Fuerza beside the Plaza de Armas has a weathervane which is used as the symbol for the famous Havana Club Rum.

Municipal de Varadero Museum

Calle 57 and Ave de la Playa
Varadero
Cell: +532 66 31 89

For an admission fee of 1CUC one can see some of the beautifully restored artifacts from that region. The wooden museum building, built nearly a century ago, is far from its glory days, but still manages to reflect the architectural style of the city. The museum has documents and pictographs depicting the original terrain of that area. It also has a collection of testimonies belonging to some of the historical figures of the city. The museum is open from Tues – Sat from 10 am – 7 pm.

Saturno Caves

Located 22 km west of Varadero, the Saturno caves were discovered accidentally by a slave in 1861 and has, over the years, become a top tourist attraction of Varadero. To get to this stalagmite cave, one has to cross over from the Varadero peninsula and drive towards Matanzas, keeping on the right. The cave is filled with cold water and makes for a good swim or snorkeling on a hot day. However one has to climb down nearly 100 steps to get in the cave and it may be a little difficult for people with walking disabilities. There is a small restaurant and bar for refreshments. One can go there as a separate tour or merge it with one of the many Jeep Safari Tours.

Gran Parque Natural Montemar

Zapata Peninsula, Matanzas

For those who want to take a break from the ocean and soak in the beauty of nature, the Great Natural Park of Montemar is the ideal getaway. It is about 150 km west of Varadero. The park is a great place to check out some of the endangered species of flora and fauna. One can also see the zunzun – one of the smallest birds in the world – and flamingoes. The park has a number of activities like scuba diving, fishing, and horseback riding. There is a museum dedicated to the historical Bay of Pigs incident. There is also a crocodile farm – Crocodile Zoocriadero.

Teatro Sauto (Sauto Theater)

Plaza de la Vigia
Matanzas
Tel: 045 24 27 21

Regarded as one of the finest theaters in Cuba, the Sauto Theater has become one of the symbols of the city. Completed in 1863, this 775 seat theater with 3 balconies was originally known as the Teatro Esteban. This neo classical architectural gem is complemented with beautiful marble statues and paintings. The floor of the theater can be raised to make it a ballroom. Declared a National Monument in 1978, the theater still hosts major events like the International Ballet Festival and Mayo Teatral.

Yumuri Day Tour (Jeep Safari)

The Yumuri Valley is located on the outskirts of the city of Matanzas. One goes past this valley while driving from Varadero or Matanzas to Havana. In fact, one of the best views of the valley is from the Bacunayagua Bridge – the highest bridge in Cuba.

During the tour, one is taken to a cove for snorkeling or a swim. There is an ecotourism trail that leads to a native village where one sees the lifestyles of the villagers. The valley has a 150 m high mountain ridge which has many vantage points to view the beautiful lush green valley. The tour also includes a visit to the caves and the coral beach. The Jeep Safari Tour is almost a 12 hr tour and costs around 75 – 90 CUC.

Casa del Ron (House of Rum)

Avenida Principal
Varadero

The 2 indulgences that people associate with Cuba are cigars and rum. Located close to calle 62, look out for the statue of the sitting devil filling a horn with rum. The House of Rum not only gives a tour of how rum is made, it also sells rum at a very reasonable government controlled price. There is also a wide variety of rums for sampling.

Recommendations for the Budget Traveler

Places to Stay

Ocean Varadero El Patriarca

Autopista Sur Km 18, Punta Hicacos, Varadero
Tel: 53 (045) 668 166
http://www.hoteloceanvaraderoelpatriarca.net/en/index.html

This 5 star seafront resort hotel is surrounded by the Varahicacos Natural Reserve.

The hotel is 34 km from the Varadero airport and 12 km from the town center of Varadero. The hotel gets its name from the 500 year old Patriarca Cactus that can be found in the beautiful gardens surrounding the property. The hotel has 420 rooms, 2 swimming pools, tennis courts, theatre, discotheque, non-motorized water sports facilities, and even a wedding gazebo. There are a number of bars and cafes.

Room rates vary from day to day and start from about € 110 for a single or double bed room.

Hotel Varadero Internacional

Ave las Americas, Km 1
Varadero
http://www.hotel-varaderointernacional.com

The Varadero International Hotel has been doing business for over half a century having opened in the 1950s. It is about 2 km from the city centre and about 30 km from the Varadero Airport. The hotel houses the famous Continental Cabaret that has featured many famous artists over the decades. The hotel is on the beach and has bars, tennis courts, and a swimming pool.

All the rooms have balconies either facing the garden or the ocean. All rooms have a safe deposit box. Room rates start from € 42 for a garden view room and € 47 for an ocean view room.

Breezes Bella Costa

Carretera de las America Km 3 1/2
Varadero
Tel: 053 45 667030
http://www.superclubscuba.com/hotel-details/Breezes-
Varadero/2000.html

Located close to the famous Varadero Golf Club, Breezes
Bella Costa is a resort hotel with special packages for
weddings. Guests must be at least 14 years of age to be in
the hotel. It has tennis courts, swimming pool, banquets,
water and land sports facilities (including diving classes
for beginners), night club, and a massage center. The hotel
has a number of restaurants and half a dozen bars in its
property.

The hotel pays for the legal expenses for a wedding if
there are at least 20 guests in the party. And, there is a
free 30 min massage for the bride and the groom! They
also have special packages for the wedded couple for
their anniversary. The property has 270 rooms. Room
rates start from around € 80 for a single person per night.

Hotel Barlovento

Ave 1rs e/10 & 12, Varadero
Tel: 5345 66 71 40

The hotel, with its colonial architecture is right at the entrance of Varadero right after crossing the Autopista Sur. The preferred location of the hotel allows it to be close to all the activities – be it the water activities or the shopping and nightlife.

The hotel is close to the famous Bar Benny and the Artex handicraft market. The hotel is about 30 km, a 40 minute ride from the airport, and 1 km from the city centre. It has a number of leisure activities for their guests.

Standard single room starts at € 50 and standard double rooms from € 73. The rooms are pool facing. During special offers and promotions there is a bottle of rum on arrival!

Blau Marina Varadero Resort

Carretera Las Morlas Final, Front of Marina Gaviota Varadero
Tel: 5345 669 966
http://www.blau-hotels-cuba.com/en/blau-marina-varadero-resort-contact.html

This hotel gets its name from the neighboring Gaviota Marina, one of the most important marinas of not only Varadero, but of Cuba.

The hotel was originally the Barceló Marina Palace; later it was bought by Blau. The hotel has a number of facilities offered to its clients including special offers during summer time like the weekly 'Beach Party' and the 'Cuba Party'. There are special wedding packages available.

There are 548 sea facing rooms. The base rate starts from € 63 for single occupancy per night.

Places to Eat & Drink

La Gruta

Josone Park
Varadero
Cell: 1418-657-0996

This is a unique restaurant inside the picturesque Josone Park where one can dine inside a cave. It has a trained English speaking staff and delicious food; specially recommended is the lobster dinner on the menu which is reasonably priced at around € 12. There is limited seating inside (one can sit outside the cave setting too), accommodating only about 20 people so it is a good idea to reserve a table before heading to the La Gruta.

Barracuda

1st Ave, Main Street
Varadero

Lookout for the giant lobster and a thatched hut on the 1st avenue at Varadero and you will be at Barracuda! There restaurant is right on the beach. One can enjoy a hearty meal here at a very reasonable price. For example, a full lobster dinner would cost around 20 pesos and would include lobster, shrimps, garlic buns, potatoes, cucumber, and coffee. There is often a Cuban band playing from one table to another. Grilled fish and lobster is recommended.

Kiki's Club

Avenida Kawama calle 5
Varadero

A touch of Italy in Cuba! Kiki's club is a small eatery specializing in Italian food – spaghetti, pizza, and all the popular Italian dishes. Of course, being in Varadero, there is the special shrimp pizza with a generous sprinkling of shrimps. It is not the most aesthetic of restaurants but the delicious food makes up for its lack in décor.

El Mojito

Via Rapida #509-A
Santa Marta, Varadero

El Mojito is a restaurant specialized in traditional Cuban cuisine and is located on the other side of the Varadero peninsula, towards the mainland. The food is delicious and very reasonably priced. However, once in the restaurant, ask for the local menu and not the tourist menu, as the tourist menu has the same food, but at a higher price! As the name of the restaurant suggests, the mojitos are the house specialty. There is also a live band.

Waco's Club

Ave 3RA E Calle 58 Y 59, 212
Varadero
Cell: 010 45 612126

Waco's Club serves an international menu. A 3 course meal with drinks and tip would cost around € 20. The restaurant is located just off the strip, about a five minute walk from the residential area of Varadero. The lobster and fish are recommended.

Places to Shop

Convention Center Plaza America

Autopista Sur km 11
Varadero
Tel: 5345 66 81 81

The Plaza America is located to the east of the Varadero Golf Club. It is the largest shopping complex in Varadero and has a number of stores along with a convention center, a mini market, a post office, and a bank. Highly recommended here is the cigar store. This is also a good place to buy clothes and souvenir items but one has to bargain for a cheaper price. There are also some food stores including a pizza store that sells reasonably priced pizza.

Bazar Cuba

cnr Av Las Américas & Calle 64 Central Varadero
Varadero

Located about halfway between the Varadero Golf Club and the Parque de Las 8000 Taquilas near Avenida Tra, this is the place to buy souvenirs and local handicrafts of Cuba as there is a huge selection to choose from. The market also has a good collection of clothing and jewelry.

La Casa Del Habano

Calle 63 y 1ra Avenida,
Varadero
Tel: 045 66 78 43
http://www.lacasadelhabano.com

The La Casa Del Habano is an international franchise that specializes in cigars. Cuba and cigars go hand in hand and this popularity of Cuban cigars has enabled the corporation to open franchises in many parts of the world including Germany, Jamaica, Mexico, and Russia. Housed in a stone building in Varadero, it has guided tours for the visitor. After the guided tour, it is expected that the guest would buy some of the cigars sold at the store.

Centro Comercial Hicacos

Parque de Las 8000 Taquilas
Varadero

In the 70s and 80s, the Parque (park) was the centre of attraction for Varadero. With changing global politics and policies, it is a mere shadow of its past. The open park has given way to plush malls. Open from 10 am to 10 pm every day the Centro Comercial Hicacos Mall has a large variety of stores selling souvenirs and local crafts. The mall also houses an Infotur office – the official tourism center.

Galeria de Arte Varadero

Ave 1 between Calle 59 and 60
Varadero

Located to the south of the Museo Minicipal Varadero, this gallery is a place to visit for those who are interested in the bourgeoisie past of Cuba. The gallery sells various items from the bourgeoisie era of Varadero like family heirlooms, paintings, and jewelry. As there is patrimony involved with these items, they are pre licensed to meet export regulations. The gallery is open from 9 am – 7 pm.

17538837R00038

Printed in Great Britain
by Amazon